THE

CRYSTAL

ORIFICE

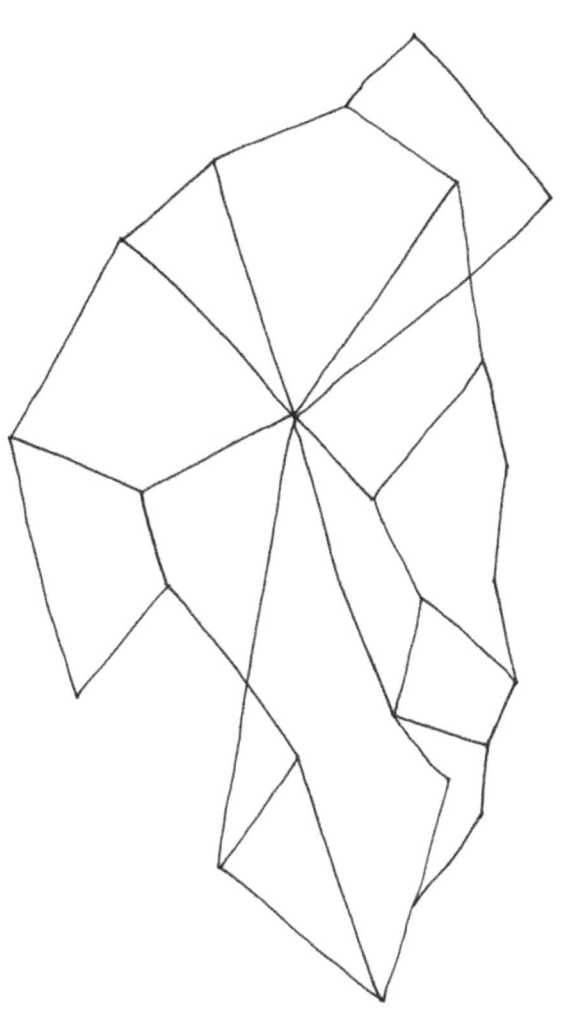

UNTITLED

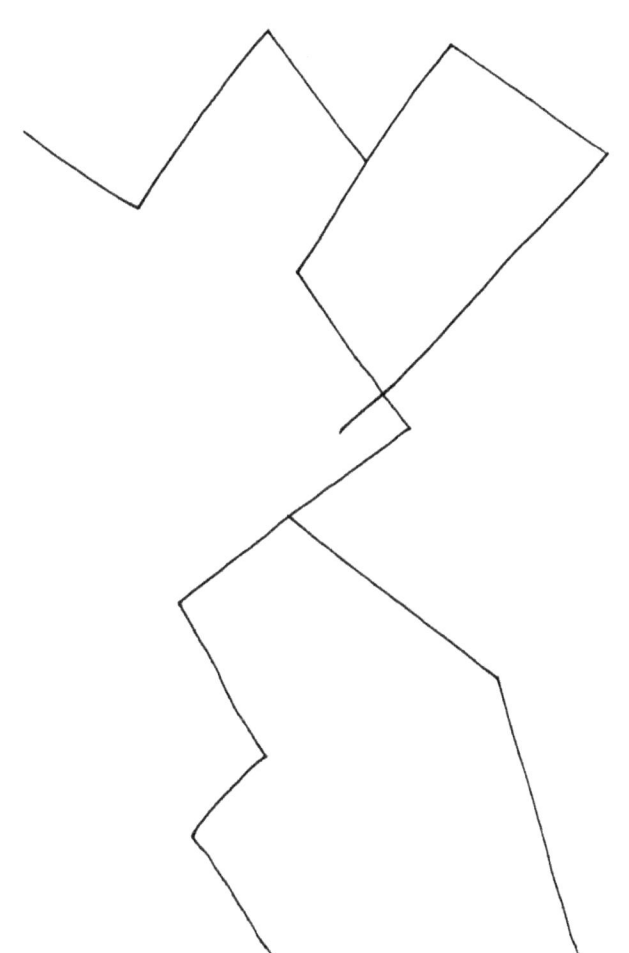

SILVER

MORNING

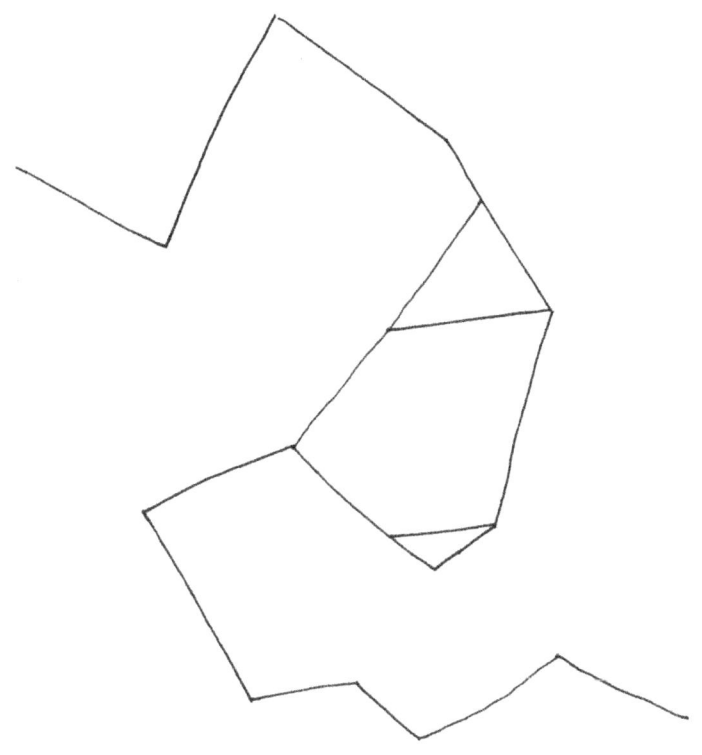

DEADPAN

GEOMETRY

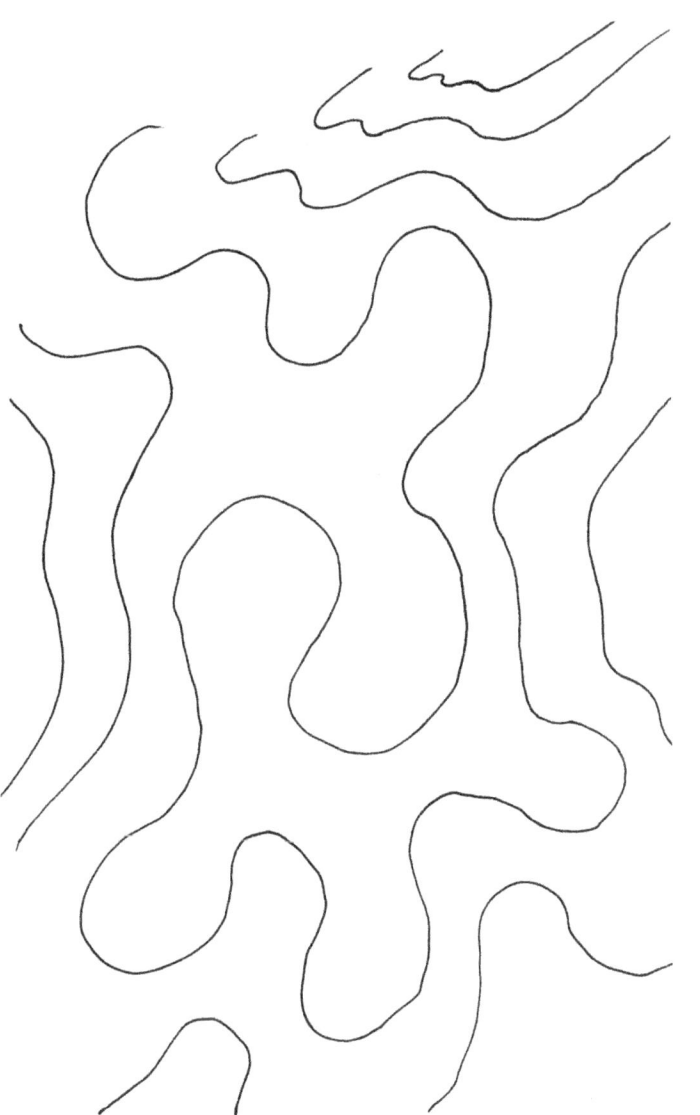

SAURON

EYELASHES

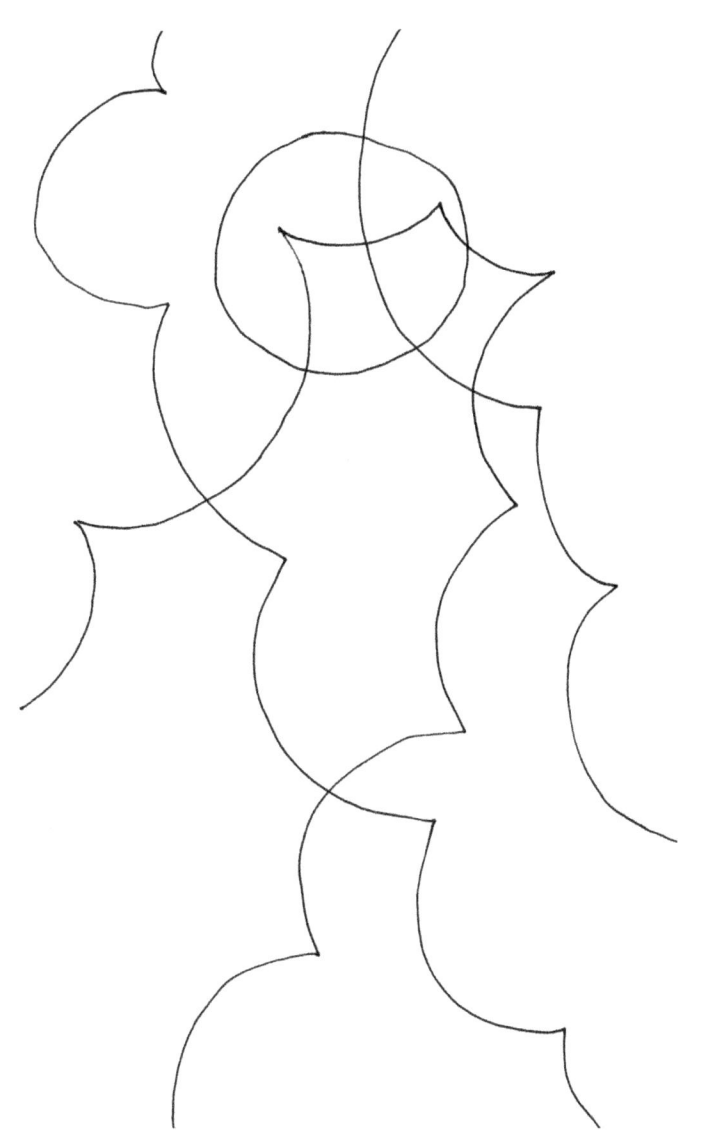

WAVE

OF

MUTILATION

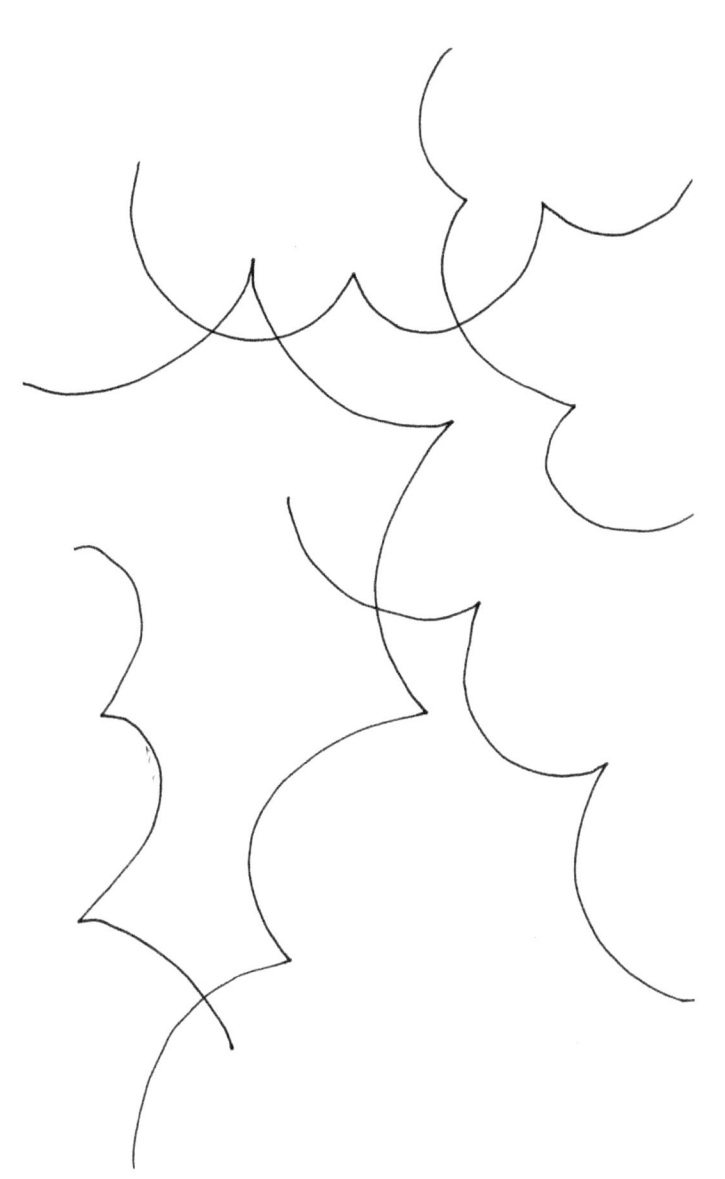

UNTITLED

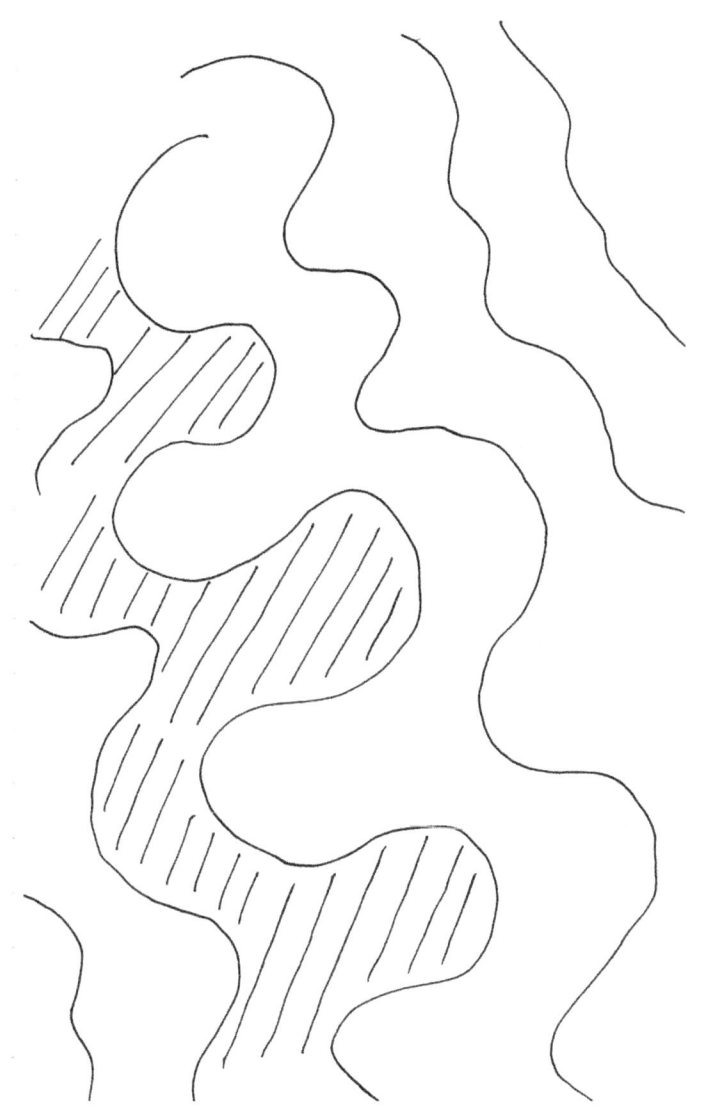

COSMIC

METABOLITE

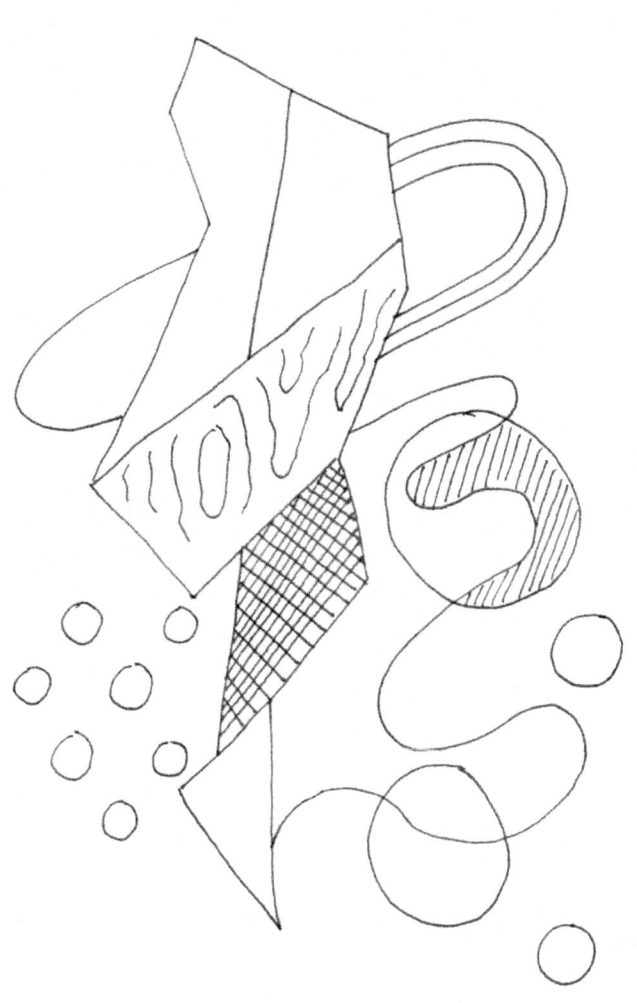

PARANORMAL

PAISLEY

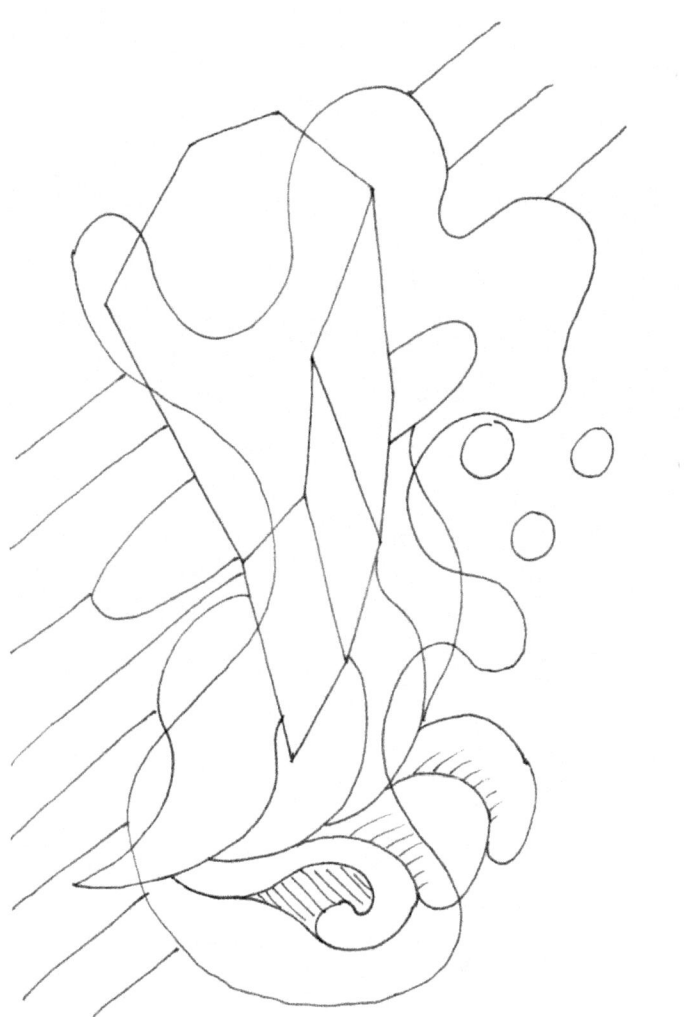

ALL IS FULL

OF LOVE

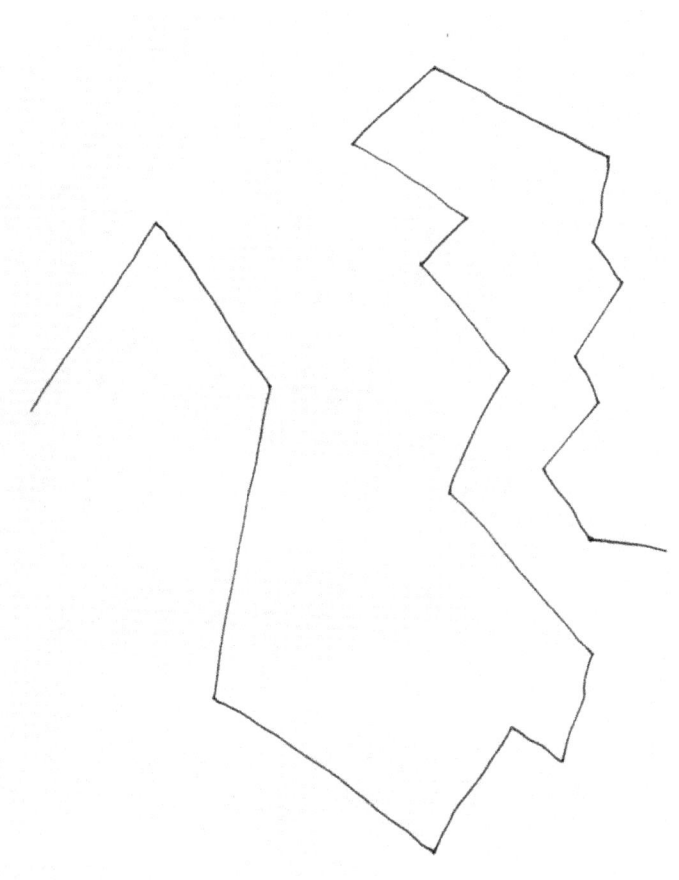

www.ingramcontent.com/pod-product-compliance
Lightning Source LLC
Chambersburg PA
CBHW072300200526
45168CB00016B/2210